Table of Contents

Foreword

I met Aaron nearly a decade ago. We were connected by a mutual friend who thought I'd be a good addition to Aaron's company, Building Cleaning Solutions. What I didn't realize at the time was that I was not just accepting a job, but rather being folded into a family, and that Aaron would ultimately become the best friend I'd ever had.

I feel truly honored that Aaron has asked me to write the foreword for his new book because there are so many people who could fill up a page with amazing words about Aaron Hudson, because he's an amazing man. Regardless of people's place or station in life, he leaves everyone with the same indelible impression. Foremost, he is a kind and generous man. He is a lover of people and has an empathetic heart. His BCS family is at the center of every business decision he makes, which means he doesn't always make the most conventional decision, but it's always the right one.

What makes him a most effective leader is the fact that he always leads by example. He is quick to take a hit for the team, long before he asks anyone else to do so. He is a man of integrity and operates his business in such a fashion that people know that if you hire BCS, you're going to get top-notch service and support.

Sure, there is a team that makes it all come together, but our success as a company is a total reflection of Aaron's heart and his vision.

He's a family man who adores his children and takes seriously his role as a father. He stewards their young lives with that perfect blend of compassion and sternness which is necessary to raise responsible and caring young adults in a chaotic world.

I'm grateful that Aaron is writing this book because he has so much to share. His heart is full with the lessons he has learned and earned over this first half of his life, and I believe they are lessons we all need to understand.

He's a true reflection of God's love and light in the world and I am incredibly grateful to call him my brother. My prayer is that you are blessed by this book and that you will likewise share it with those you know who might need a little love and light in their life as well.

By his grace,
Steve Burton

Introduction

I have one simple reason for writing this book. To make sure you are equipped with a proper (in my well researched opinion) and sustainable concept of being a Christ follower. I want to equip you with a sound theology to guide you through a more enjoyable and life changing experience through studying the absolute awesomeness of the Bible. I will try to give you a 30,000 foot view of common denominators that bind the Bible from Genesis to Revelations that are sustainable and indisputable (truly by almost anyone) [*even* a chosen lunatic mentality]!

There will be many times, if you read this book in its entirety, that you will be confused, frustrated and possibly argumentative. I encourage all of those emotions. Anything emotional that this book invokes, I believe will prompt you to dig deeper, which will uncover truth/peace.

I believe that whenever you get Law and Grace preached in unequal scales, you rapidly go down the road of "cult" as opposed

1

to sustainable theology. There are currently more cults than religions in our world today. The Western world is especially guilty of unbalancing the scale due to our consumer culture lifestyles.

Showing my cynical side now…I believe the reason for this is the necessity of the "guilt" message in order to increase tithing. I don't think Jesus really wanted these big buildings and the massive financial resources they demand in order keep them running. I am sure I am not surprising anyone with the thought of how many people around the world could use the money for food and the basic introduction to Jesus. An introduction to Jesus takes love and community, not buildings. For centuries the guilt message has been used to give people the feeling (albeit implied) that they could tithe their way back, or into, God's grace. The truth is that you are never out of it. The only variable is how you receive it. In addition to the biblical fact that 10% tithing is not mentioned in the New Testament…II Corinthians 8 basically says: Love your neighbor by helping them out, not just financially. Every aspect of doing for others is considered tithing from a biblical aspect. In fact, the whole idea of tithing in the Old Testament was agrarian, or land and harvest. The concept of giving 10% of your salary is simply a made up concept to put names on pews and wings of churches that are empty six days a week. The reference in Hebrews (perhaps the most often taken out of context as a guilt message) concerning Abraham giving 10% to Melchizedek was based on plunder from war. The Bible almost never (with very few exceptions) relates tithing to money. Don't get me wrong; tithing is essential to a Christian...time, talent and most of all love! The fact is, when you truly understand what has been done for you, it should happen automatically, as Paul refers to in II Corinthians 8. Christians should focus on filling needs of others and not percentages. Love meets a much more important need than money.

In C.S. Lewis's book, *Abolition of Man,* he points out that every mainstream religion shares seven of the Ten Commandments. The ones it does not share makes all of the difference in peace and freedom, which Christ offered us through his sacrifice. All religions basically say work hard at being good and maybe you will live in paradise. Jesus says the kingdom is within you. I have paid the price for sin once and for all -- now how do you respond to that? I will cover Grace and Mercy in later chapters, but remember this: Revelations 3:20, I knock at the door of your heart...will you answer?

The primary motivation for writing this book is for my three amazing children: Lauren, Caitlin, and Tre (Aaron Hudson III). Through my younger years, basically until I met my wife when I was 30, I had fire insurance but no real understanding of being a Christ follower. I can tell you without hesitation, it is like having a winning lottery ticket versus turning the lottery ticket in for the cash. Both are victories, but one is unarguably more satisfying than the other.

Without question, the turning point of my walk was December 4, 2007. I had taken my kids to our boat on Lake Lanier the evening before for a routine sleepover. On the way home, roughly 9:45 am, I got a phone call from my best friend's wife telling me that he had died *(against my better judgment, I have changed his name in this book – although I have acquiesced at the request of his wife and children, I hope they do not miss the fact that this was God's plan)*. Mike was - without a rival - the best friend I had ever known. Given the fact that I moved around a lot as a child, i.e. many different schools and no real roots in any given city, Mike was the closest friend I ever had.

I met Mike while I was Activities Director at Georgian Bay Apartments in Fort Myers. Mike was moving over from Miami and wanted to see an apartment layout, and mine was the only one we could show. I was a Golf Professional at Gateway Golf and Country Club at the time, and paired with his love for golf, an instant friendship was developed.

Mike was raised (and due to a couple of divorces) as "the man" of the house. He loved and took great care of his mother Carol and sister Stephanie. However, the rough visual of marriage and heartache left Mike with a distaste for ever getting married and a basic, although not studied, atheistic view of God.

To shorten a long story…Mike did in fact soften over the years and met his wife Marla. Shortly after they got married they moved to Windermere, Florida and Mike became a father for the first time. As children do, I saw Faith melt his heart into a useable condition. Marla became pregnant again with Hope, whom Mike would never get to meet. He had everything and his future was bright; and it was all lost due to one really bad decision while at a local house party celebrating the Virginia Tech vs. Florida State football game. He was living in a very affluent neighborhood and hanging out with young, rich yuppies who had an appetite for unhealthy consumption, which in this case, was cocaine. Mike knew he had minor heart issues, and as it turns out they were exaggerated by the use of cocaine the night of his death.

His heart could not handle it.

The last year of his life, no less than weekly, we would wind up on the phone and the conversation would end with me telling him to research his faith. I remember countless great questions that he would use to oppose Christianity where I would simply say…"I don't know, but I will find out and call you back". This not only forced me to learn more about what I professed, but it was a blatant reminder that I had little more than fire insurance at the time. Mike was making steps (faster than I was) and starting to see glimmers of spiritual light, but died before he could truly grasp the reality that Jesus was the author of hope. I will never forget, as long as I live, the feeling I had the months and year or two after his death of…absolute failure. I remember praying for forgiveness for failing to know more about the realities of Jesus and theology that would have prevented Mike from living a hopeless life. I vowed to never fail another friend or person due to laziness and lack of studying that would make the faith I have indisputable, defendable and worthwhile.

II Timothy 2:15
Do your best to present yourself to God as one approved, a worker who does not need to be ashamed and who correctly handles the word of truth.

I have, for the past six years, been on a reading and studying tear! I have read and studied more in the past six years than the previous 40 by a large margin. I have studied history, genetics, evolution, philosophy and most importantly, theology. Although I do not claim to be an expert at any of them, I believe the unbiased mind that I approached all of these categories with, will greatly enable me to speak more intelligently about what I believe with every morsel of my being. I also trust that it is sustainable for anyone who reads it.

From my late teens to age 30 I was a tennis professional. At The Racquet Club of Pittsburgh, I worked primarily with tournament level juniors. In 1988 I helped three different girls get college scholarships to major universities. In 1988 I moved to Florida where I worked for a year at Rick Macci's Academy. At Macci's I had the opportunity to work with, in small part, Jennifer Capriati, Tommy Ho, Vimmel Patel and Michelle Rae Rodgers, who I later travelled with to several Junior National events as a private coach.

In 1993, I decided to enter the Professional Golf Association Apprentice program. I passed my Players Ability Test at The Vineyards in Naples, Florida in 1994, with my Dad caddying (which was priceless). In 1995, I decided to go back to the tennis profession and took over a small tennis facility just outside Fort Myers, Florida.

I met Rebecca in Hong Kong when I was interviewing for a tennis/golf professional job. She was an au pair for one of the kids in one of my "interview lessons" on my first trip to Hong Kong, and the reason why I accepted the job. I married Rebecca in Hong Kong December 4th, 1996. We stayed in Hong Kong until August of 1997, just after the historic handover to China, ending the 100 Year Lease (quite an experience).

In 1998, while my wife was pregnant with our first daughter Lauren, I took a job with ABM. ABM is an international building maintenance company, specializing in commercial janitorial services. My first assignment was in Birmingham, Alabama. Within 18 months I helped bring a losing operation to profitability and then was promoted to a post in Atlanta. While managing ABM Atlanta, we went from losing $56,000 a month to profitable in roughly nine months (on roughly $24M in annualized sales). It was then I figured out that *I was not meant for corporate work.*

After leaving ABM I took one more commercial janitorial management position in Atlanta at REDLEE, SCS. REDLEE was a much smaller operation, which I thought would offer me more latitude, but did not. I worked with REDLEE for nine months, again helping a desperately losing operation to increased profitability and success.

In July 2001, the month my second daughter, Caitlin, was born, I launched Building Cleaning Solutions, Inc. I am happy to say, by God's sustaining grace, it is my work today.

Before launching this book, I have to add one more side bar, my call to ministry. This is a very hard thing to explain, but those of you that can discern the difference between you telling yourself what you want God's will to be, and feeling in your heart what God's will is...know it is very different.

I was engaged at a small church in Woodstock, Georgia. I played guitar and sometimes drums for the praise team band. One Sunday morning before church, I went outside to pray and I remember saying (which I strongly discourage praying unless you are ready to move); God, I want to do more. I want you to use my unique fingerprint to positively affect your children. I was not prepared for what came next. After playing our first song, *Let it Rise*, a Big Daddy Weave cover, our Pastor introduced the Head Chaplain of the Cherokee County jail. He told a little bit about what he did for the jail and its inmates and said there was a need for pastors. My head slowly descended to my guitar with tears in my eyes...I was touched...and things would not ever be the same again. In 2009, I entered the chaplain program, became ordained online in 2010, and have been ministering to young men in the maximum security portion of the jail for the past five years.

Since I will not be formally footnoting this book, I would like to offer the following as my primary influences: The Bible (various versions); C.S. Lewis (*Mere Christianity, Abolition of Man, Problem of Pain, Four Loves, Screwtape Letters,* and many others); Timothy Keller (*The Reason for God: Belief in an Age of Skepticism, The Prodigal God)*, and countless sermons; Andy Stanley's countless sermons; Francis Collins, who decoded the human genome in 1995, (*The Language of God: A Scientist Presents Evidence for Belief*); Karen Armstrong (*A History of Christianity*); Eusebius of Caesarea (*The Church History*); John Owen (*The Mortification of Sin,* circa 1700); Phillip Johnson (*Darwin on Trial*); one of my favorites, hard to read for emotional reasons, Viktor Frankl (*Man's Search for Meaning*); in addition to many more both secular and Christ based books and peripheral studies.

Finally I would like to add this: I make no excuses for the rawness of this book. It will not be edited for content, but just for the basics. My editor will work on spelling, syntax & format etc. It will have cut and pastes (not plagiary), as I fully admit I can hardly trace an original thought of my own. The grammar may be incorrect at best, but that is who I am. I do strive for perfection knowing I won't reach it, knowing that while striving I will at least improve. However, what you will see is "Where I Am and Who I Am".

Philippians 4:7
Peace that transcends understanding [to all that read this book].

Son or Lunatic

Well let's start with the center of everything. In C.S. Lewis' most famous book, *Mere Christianity*, he asks this simple question: Either Jesus was the Son of God or a stark raving lunatic, which do you really believe?

"I am trying here to prevent anyone saying the really foolish thing that people often say about Him: I'm ready to accept Jesus as a great moral teacher, but I don't accept his claim to be God. That is the one thing we must not say. A man who was merely a man and said the sort of things Jesus said would not be a great moral teacher. He would either be a lunatic — on the level with the man who says he is a poached egg — or else he would be the Devil of Hell. You must make your choice. Either this man was, and is, the Son of God, or else a madman or something worse. You can shut him up for a fool, you can spit at him and kill him as a demon or you can fall at his feet and call him Lord and God, but let us not

come with any patronizing nonsense about his being a great human teacher. He has not left that open to us. He did not intend to." - C.S. Lewis

I love the strength of this stance! However, if you research the history of Jesus Christ as a strictly historical figure, you will find where C.S. Lewis found these factual grounds to plant a stake. You see, no secular historian (worth his or her keep!) would ever deny the fact that Jesus was in fact a historical figure. The variance comes when you decide to ponder the question, "who" is he? If he was a great teacher, then his teachings would have stood on their own merits, and one could safely assume he would have left them as just that...teachings. Muhammad and Buddha were both great teachers (with human limitations). However, if you would have asked Muhammad if he was God...he would have had you killed immediately for the very insinuation. If you had asked Gautama Buddha the same question he would have said..."God? I am looking for absolute transcendence, a way to master the mind and body. I am not God, my philosophies should be followed, but I am not my philosophy."

However, Jesus said:

John 14:1-7
[1] "Do not let your hearts be troubled. You believe in God; believe also in me. [2] My Father's house has many rooms; if that were not so, would I have told you that I am going there to prepare a place for you? [3] And if I go and prepare a place for you, I will come back and take you to be with me that you also may be where I am. [4] You know the way to the place where I am going." [5] Thomas said to him, "Lord, we don't know where you are going, so how can we know the way?" [6] Jesus answered, "I am the way and the truth and the life. No one comes to the Father except through me. [7] If you really know me, you will know my Father as well. From now on, you do know him and have seen him."

Through elementary eyes you can deduce that he was NOT speaking metaphorically. Jesus plainly said, if you have seen me you have seen the Father, or God. Wow! Great teacher? Or Emanuel?

17

Timeout for context update: Remember, Jesus as a child would have been raised up in a Jewish tradition, memorizing the Old Testament and its teachings. These traditions would have included the incredible reverence for the word Yahweh or YhWh. The scribes of the time could not even say the word out loud for fear of being irreverent. The word basically means "I Am". Remember what he said to Moses at the burning bush… "I am that I am". It would be IMPOSSIBLE for any Jew to put himself in the position of Emanuel (God with us) without knowing he would be immediately excommunicated, or killed. This would have been, and to the Pharisees was, blasphemy. Had Jesus been a Greek, one might argue the context could be taken metaphorically. Greeks were considered the more philosophical of the two. Jews were deeply physical and "Law" oriented whereas Greeks would have been more "Spirit of the Law", and analogy oriented. We will dive deeper in Chapter 5, Consumer God, where I write about Physics vs. Spirit.

Furthermore, Jesus said he could not only forgive you of your sins, but also your sins against others? *Hello*! Son or Lunatic?

Now I really want to offend some people here…

If you are a professed Atheist, which by default would be of the judgment that Jesus was perhaps just a lunatic, you are, in my opinion, pathetically lazy and most assuredly have taken the path of least resistance. You see, **if** you have in fact studied your position…you have either checked your brain at the door (admittedly the majority of Christians do the same) or only studied to prove what you were looking for and stopped there. I believe wholeheartedly that in order to find the truth you have to be able to identify falsities. Short of this you are simply being brainwashed or brainwashing yourself, or worse yet, letting institutions (with agendas) tell you what to think.

It is extremely important that I reiterate this disclaimer: Jesus is not Religion! There are roughly 21 mainstream religions ranging from Christianity (2.1 billion), Islam (1.3 billion), Hindu

(1 billion), all the way to Rastafarian (600,000), etc. There is a simple formula that determines a religion: (circle of influence + truth claim = religion). Again, you might remember the verse John 14:6 mentioned earlier. Jesus was the incarnation and the epicenter of truth.

Atheism originated from the Greek ἄθεος (atheos), meaning "without god(s)". It was circa 18th century when this movement started referring to themselves as Atheist, or not believing in any Gods or deities. One way of looking at it is in order to profess Atheism you have to either walk past any rational thought about "where did we come from…?" or embrace the theory of evolution.

I have opened Pandora's Box with the mentioning of Charles Darwin who is the author of the theory of evolution (through natural selection). In other words…evolution by the strongest genes winning out. He penned this theory while studying the Galapagos Islands. One of the foundational premises of his theory was the evolution of the study of the Galapagos Finch. He noted that the finches changed over time thus giving him the idea that we are all creatures evolving through time. In his famous book, *The Origin of Species*, he does however note: "Organs of extreme Perfection and Complication. To suppose that the eye with all its inimitable contrivances for adjusting the focus to different distances, for admitting different amounts of light, and for the correction of spherical and chromatic aberration, could have been formed by natural selection, seems, I freely confess, absurd in the highest degree."

Let's start with a completely developed, fully functioning eye (the only kind that has ever been found!) and work backward a couple of evolutionary steps and you will see why Darwin was so candid. Take away just one of the "evolved" parts of the eye, let's say the retina, and what do you have? An organ that can see? Hardly! Subtract the lens, or the cornea. Then put the retina back. Could the eye see? Never! It must be complete or it won't function.

By what reasoning or logic, then, would an eyeless creature begin a hundred-million-year project of forming an eye, which would be of no use to it whatsoever until the hundred million years were over? Did these microscopic animals think they were developing something that would be useful after a period of time of which humans cannot even begin to conceive? And how many more million years for a fish eye to evolve to be useful out of water?

Of course the scientific world would rather table that and focus on the "illusions" of the obvious that helps attract the oblivious. These two mentalities are similar for a reason!

For a more intelligent and more in depth view of this point (as I can't do all of your homework for you...), read the book, *Darwin on Trial*, by Phillip Johnson.

One short note on the other, I might add, extremely intelligent argument against the Bible and its claims...Old earth vs. Young earth. In short I will ask you one rather sarcastic question, but one you need to battle with if you wish to promote the Old earth theory. Was Adam born a man or an infant? A Man! If God created Adam as a fully developed man, would it not make sense that he made earth fully developed to sustain his story, or History? Visit answersingenesis.com for further education on this subject matter as it is well above my intelligence level.

Scientific institutions rely heavily on grant money. This was not always the case. Many of the greatest scientists in the history of the world did their research on their own nickel. Galileo, Newton, Franklin, Einstein and Charles Darwin all worked to afford the ability to exercise their scientific dreams. The reason I mention this is that when you are free to think without strings you will by human nature perhaps be less biased in your pursuits. For example, many college professors have been fired or blacklisted for simply mentioning intelligent design as the origin of the universe. Many financiers have basically placed "No God allowed" policies for the money they have given in order to study the origins of life and earth. How can you have scientific achievement if you limit other theories? The Latin word science means knowledge. How can you possibly know what the world looks like if you are isolated in Miami? Your truth is not truth at all; it is simply the proving of your environment.

More people convert to Christianity while trying to disprove the Bible than ever find traction for their original intent. Two of my favorite examples are C.S. Lewis and Lee Stroebel. Lee was a Chicago journalist and involved in some pretty major crime cases. His wife felt like something was missing in her life, and like many of us…she went to church to find it. She became more and more active in church and Lee became a little jealous and basically looked at her new found religion as a crutch. He then decided he would use his journalistic talents to investigate Jesus in order to show his wife this was not the answer. You can read the book for yourself, *The Case for Christ,* if you want the whole story, but Lee Stroebel gave his life to Jesus and now teaches his research around the country to Christians (and Atheists) alike. If you question Jesus, this is a must read book.

C.S. Lewis, by far, is one of my biggest inspirations to this date. C.S. Lewis entered Oxford University as a devout atheist. He became roommates with a couple of well-educated Christians and this set "Jack's", as known by his friends, mind ablaze. Jack lost his mother to cancer at a young age and the very concept of a good God letting bad exist simply defied his young mind's reason. C.S. Lewis was at Oxford with J.R.R Tolkien. I find this amazing and simply God arranged! Think of just the secular (with Bible stories wisely interwoven throughout) books (and movies) these cats would later put out *Lord of the Rings, Chronicles of Narnia,* etc.... Wow! Jack, being the deep thinker that he is, simply would not let his proclaimed atheism go unchecked. Lewis' conversations and arguments with J.R.R. Tolkien about theology and the reality of God and Jesus are largely to blame for his returning to faith and becoming, in my opinion, the greatest apologetic Christian mind of all time. Please read the book, based on a series of radio addresses during World War II, called, *Mere Christianity*. Take your time with this book...there is nothing in it that does not make you look inward.

PACC = HELL

I freely admit that this chapter is largely borrowed and embellished from a wonderful sermon, later revised into a book from an 18th century theologian by the name of John Owen. In his book titled *The Mortification of Sin,* Owen seemed to think that being able to delineate the differences between physical actions and spiritual feelings were essential in understanding spiritual growth. Of course we all know the passage in the book of James 2, where he made the analysis "…faith without works is dead, and works without faith is dead".

There are four major categories that all physical or earthly pursuits fall into, and an equal number of categories that spiritual pursuits fall into. For the physical (earthly) there is the need for Power, Acceptance, Control and Comfort. Conversely, for the spiritual they are Grace, Mercy, Submission and Vulnerability.

Romans 12:2

Do not conform to the patterns of this world, but be transformed by the renewing of your mind.

In the physical world in which you are fed constantly there is the insinuated need for increased measures of Power, Acceptance, Control and Comfort. In the front of my Bible there are two significant sticky notes that I try to read (even though I have memorized them) each time I open my bible. The one I am writing about now is my favorite and most difficult to accept: "The need for Power, Acceptance, Control and Comfort leads to Hell".

Power is achieved by creating divisions and levels (the highest level garnering the most power). Once you have the highest level in any organization established there is the constant need for competing with the next person for that position. Throughout this type of leadership design, there is, on all levels, the intended by-product of competition that thrives on the natural mentality of self-actualization. I would be better, and considered better by others, if I could achieve…

In the book, *The Church History,* by Eusebius of Caesarea, 3rd century Christian historian (later translated in the 1970's), he wrote, "...most of the concept of equal, which was the premise of Jesus' message, had been pushed aside as the church reestablished levels of priesthood". This to me was amazing. Only 300 years later, man had decided once again to separate himself by the illusion of power, and in this case, clothes and wealth.

In the USA we currently have (as of this writing) an administration that makes laws and changes laws in order to "level the playing field".

The simple -- however catastrophic problem here -- is its lack of spiritual understanding. You see we are all created equal, not the same! For example, in war you have men that are on the front lines, then you have officers that direct them. Could you imagine only Officers without Soldiers? Another example is all Chiefs and no Indians? You see they are not the same, but equally important. Another example is a baseball team. The pitcher makes $6M a year, and the center fielder makes $400K a year. How good is the pitcher if someone makes a hit to centerfield and there is no one there? They are not the same, but work together to create the whole, which is the true value. I could go on, but I think you get my concept.

When Jesus led, he never led through Power. In the first century, power was defined by possessions much like today. The more land, animals and servants you had the more power.

Matthew 8:20
Foxes have dens and Rabbits have holes, but the son of man has nowhere to lay his head.

Instead of using conventional Power to gain a following, Jesus used Influence, which we will get to later. He lived a very poor and meager existence but yet was followed in droves and still is the most influential and controversial leader to date.

I remember talking to a client about ministering in jail. My client said "I can't believe you talk to these murderers, thieves and child molesters and not want to kill them". My reply was simple: They have not done anything that I am not capable of doing under their exact environmental circumstances. I am blessed that God did not see necessary for me to have their childhood, and his plan was different for me. But I am not better, just different. I remember the following from a leadership conference from Zig Ziglar:

"There is no such thing as a person being better or worse than another, only a person with a different set of circumstances. I am willing to bet that there are 1.5 billion people under the age of 8 that can do something that nobody in this room can do… Speak Chinese! Does that make them better? Does that make them different with a different set of circumstances?"

I believe at the core of the Christian message lies this very simple, but far from simplistic concept. We are all equal, just not the same.

Acceptance is a funny one. The need for acceptance or approval is really one of the driving emotions behind the power problem. We use our personal relationships to weave our way into circles that we would not normally be in through piecing together relationships like a puzzle. All this manipulating and posturing is to gain social acceptance, often at the cost of our souls.

How about this: you do not wear what you want to wear, only what other people wear, and they set the standards of acceptance. I was in Iowa speaking to a group of 105 foster kids. At the end of my sermon I noticed two girls about 16 years old wanted to talk to me, one on one. As we began to talk they expressed how difficult it was for them to be poor and not have the clothes the other kids had. They told me that the other kids constantly ridiculed them for their out of style clothes and worn out shoes. Maddy told me that during P.E. one day the other "popular" girls actually took her shirt and threw it in the mud and Maddy had to wear it the rest of the day. I cried with them. The other girl asked me, "Where is God in this?" I replied, right there with you. I went on to tell them that their behavior was sustainable, but the mean girls' was not. You see, the other girls were propping up their social status by their parents' ability to buy them nice clothes, while their status was being elevated by their dependence on God. God will always win in the long run, and a lot of times even in the short run, you just have to keep your eyes and thoughts on heaven and not earth. Those mean girls were living a facade. They were living on everything but their own attributes, works and achievements. This popularity is simply not sustainable.

In the 1990's I wrote this poem:

"A facade is like another world,
A world we know nothing about,
Something we all want to be,
When we are frightened of what we really are,
Why we want another world?
When we can't fix the one we have.
All these vicious cycles,
Just create a pain in the ASS!"

Fueled by the need for acceptance, approval and the gaining of power will enable us to do things that, in hindsight, we are often ashamed of actually. When our central concern is self-actualization, there is nothing most of us won't do.

Another great example of the continued social decay in this arena is the following. In 1995 a Cornell professor created a 200-question test with a few strategic questions buried, that would give a current moral metric of his graduating class. His motive was to determine what percentage of his class would lie, cheat or say something untrue about a co-worker to get ahead. In 1995 the number of people that would immorally advance their career was 31%. That seems to me like a very high number. However the real problem comes when he hands out the same questionnaire in 2006, just 11 years later. The number climbs to 67%. My belief is that we have created such a poisonous social environment that we as a country measure ourselves by the amount of power and acceptance we have instead of the way in which we achieve it.

I find myself constantly praying that my plans work out, and everything is the way I think it should be. Funny, huh? This is my (very ugly) control issue. I think that I am smart enough to know what is best for me and that my plan should be sold to my creator and he should then grant my perfect plan so that I can wake up tomorrow and walk gently down the road of least resistance, my road! The problem here is the ridiculously simple plan I have. How could my God grant such a plan that does not include certain people that I need to get to know in order to bless and be blessed by? However, the minute things do not work out the way that I think a good God should work them out, I get frustrated and feel abandoned. I have seen my control issues face to face.

I am currently going through marriage issues unlike anything I could have ever thought of or foreseen. I am certainly not going to paint myself a victim. With even a small amount of thought I realize that I would take my problems over 99% of those on earth, but it still hurts. I have been accused of affairs, hiding money and a constant assault on my integrity. I can say without hesitation, none of these accusations are the least bit warranted or remotely true. Because of my deeply sensitive nature, I have often said "…her I might be able justify cheating on, but it would be my children that would pay the collateral debt." I simply would never let that happen. I remember about five weeks ago going outside to pray and found myself frustrated with God. I was crying out (literally) saying why are you doing this to me? I remember a prayer that went something like this:

Father I want to be grateful for all you have done, but right now I am broken in a puddle of nothing on the floor. I see no evidence that you hear me or even care (I cried). I am sorry Father but you know my heart, and I can't pretend in front of you. I am not man enough and my faith is not strong enough to continue to take this assault on my love and faithfulness to my marriage. I have taken all I can at the hands of a woman that I love beyond words. Everything I have done is for nothing. I can't do this anymore! (The tears continued)…

As I was quiet for a moment, I literally was feeling worse. I was thinking…I just cried and complained to the one who has blessed me in so many ways telling my Father that it still was not enough, I needed…no I deserved (consumer God) a great marriage too. I knew in my mind I was wrong, but my heart was consumed with pain that I have never felt before. In that moment, another quiet moment, a picture went through my mind of teaching Lauren, my oldest, how to ride a bicycle. I saw the memory of being in front of the house (you could see the dinner table from where we were) holding the back of the bike trying to get her to just trust the bike would stay upright. We must have been there for over an hour. Rebecca actually was frustrated that I would not stop and eat, as dinner was ready. Finally Lauren said, "Let go, I got it." Funny thing…I already had about 40 yards earlier. She was riding! Once she released her illusion of control and trusted the bike, she was unstoppable. I then realized I was not in a puddle on the floor, I was simply growing through this enormous pain. God had me then, as he does now.

My point is, that without facing obstacles you can't get over yourself, you are left to your own control. Control itself is an illusion. The truth is, you control nothing! Everything that you think you control is simply you limiting God to try and stay safe. I was doing that exact thing through my marriage. It was not what I needed, but how do I know what God needs to do in her? I know that without this, my faith would not have grown. I was becoming stagnant. Pain is necessary if you want to grow and there is no place for control. If you need to control, then you don't need God. In the end, there are two types of people, those who believe in God, or those that are their own god.

Finally…comfort issues! Wow, the things we use to find comfort! I often tell people that we are all addicts. Some of us are addicted to conventional things like drugs or alcohol but most of us are addicted to less criticized and more socially acceptable things like money, popularity, religion, fame, social status, our bodies (workout addicts) etc…the rub is in the definition of addiction; which is the need of more and more in order to achieve the same effect.

My favorite analogy to this is: everyone is a ladder. You see, a ladder only has value when it is propped up against something.

When it leans on something it then has definition. It might be a 6 foot ladder or a 24 foot ladder, but its stability is only when it is on something. Again, some people put their ladder on their jobs, their wife's or husband's beauty, their car, the size of their house, their children's success in school, etc. The problem comes in two forms, one is simple…someone always has more; therefore your ladder hits the floor! The other problem is the proof of how little we control in these physical arenas. What happens when you lose your job? What happens when your straight A child gets into trouble? Your ladder comes crashing to the floor.

Wayne Dyer did a program called "Change Your Thoughts Change Your Life". He spoke of the Tao Te Ching throughout this program. It is a very interesting read and I strongly encourage checking it out. One of the chapters hit me square between the eyes. It said in short that happiness is not in having more, but being truly content with less. It is a fact that of the 100% of the clothes in your closet you only wear about 20%. The remaining 80% are simply there for comfort. He told a great story about his son and daughter-in-law and two children coming to visit him and his wife in Maui, Hawaii that illustrated this concept while teaching his son this very virtue.

Dr. Dyer asked his son, "What is your favorite t-shirt?" His son replied; "The one I am wearing." Dr. Dyer replied; "Take the shirt off and give it to me." His son said, "No, I am not going to give you my favorite t-shirt (smiling)." Dr. Dyer said again, "Give me your t-shirt." His son again replied; "Dad, I am not going to give you my favorite t-shirt, I have had it for years and I love it." Dr. Dyer replied; "Son, I am your Dad, I want that t-shirt" (smugly but becoming more serious). His son finally relented, knowing full well there was a lesson lurking, and gave up his favorite t-shirt. Dr. Dyer proceeded to wear that t-shirt every day, taking it off only to wash it, for the next 15 days…His son repeatedly, sometimes tense but always yielding to the knowledge that there was a lesson in here somewhere, asked if he could have his t-shirt back as his father was wearing it out. Finally his son asked the important question… "Dad when are you going to give me back my favorite t-shirt?" and Dr. Dyer replied; "Son, I will give you back your t-shirt when you are truly happy you gave it to me." You see the comfort of that t-shirt became painfully clear when he had to face it every day. By facing it every day he was able to break free of the need for something so trivial.

One of my favorite examples of our terminal need for comfort is our habits. Again, back to what I call addictions. We are creatures of habits and perpetually, sub-consciously look for habits in order to gain control and more importantly comfort. In a really cool leadership book called *The Servant* by James Hunter, he referred to routines as ruts… He proceeded to explain that ruts are simply coffins with the head and feet pushed out. I really enjoyed that visual.

One of the greatest and most impressive men I have met in my life, I also have the pleasure of working with in my company. He repeatedly says that he hates when things are calm and comfortable. He knows full well the alluring affect that comfort can draw you into stagnation, gluttony, comfort, sloth etc…

Again, the earth is pulling you into the arenas of power, acceptance, control and comfort on a never-ending basis. If you are awake, you are being pulled. The most important thing you can do is to be aware and fight for your spiritual health by taking one battle at a time and never relenting. Even if you feel like you are losing, your God is bigger and more able than you can possibly imagine.

EGG

In the previous chapter I pointed out the relentless pursuit that the earth has for your soul. The earth/Satan has a desperate need to convince you that life on earth is the end game. Everything that you are taught to pursue is aimed at first convincing yourself that you live…you die…and that is it. This is where you really have to be honest with yourself. If you believe this life is the end game then:

1 Corinthians 15:32
If I fought wild beasts in Ephesus with no more than human hopes, what have I gained? If the dead are not raised, "Let us eat and drink, for tomorrow we die."

First let me back up, as I have opened Pandora's Box with the mention of Satan. If you don't believe in Satan then, in my opinion, you cannot believe in God. You cannot pick and choose portions of the Bible to believe in and create some sort of a la carte religion. Well, I guess you can, but it again will never be sustainable. Satan exists and rules this earth. He knows the Bible better than you do and he uses tactics that are all centered on getting you to make earth more important than your thoughts and aspirations for heaven. In the book, *Screwtape Letters,* from C.S. Lewis, he illustrates several ways that Satan is at work. I, again, strongly encourage reading this book.

So, how do we separate ourselves from the earthly pull of power, acceptance, control and comfort; *and* feed our spirit with the fuel necessary to battle these daily? EGG!

Before I explain the EGG concept let me briefly explain what sustainable and unsustainable growth is. At a youth program at my former church, at the end of the program the pastor came up and did the prayer of salvation. He told anyone that was moved tonight to pray this prayer. "Lord I repent of my sins, I acknowledge you as my Lord and Savior and freely invite you to be my Lord and Savior". Much to my shock I saw Lauren and Caitlin repeating this prayer. I knew they accepted Jesus Christ as their Savior at least two years earlier as it is a staple conversation in our house, as you can imagine. Later that week I went upstairs to talk to Lauren about her relationship with Jesus and why she felt she had to accept him again, as he already accepted her? She said, they always do that and she just felt she was supposed to go along with it. Ouch! We have a church looking for head count while leaving spirits stranded in search of the next exoterical experience to tie them over. *Houston we have a problem*! I asked her what her thoughts were on accepting Jesus and she said there was supposed to be some life changing thing that never happened, so she was confused and thought it did not happen. I remember smiling, while thanking God for the courage to investigate, and giving her this analogy: When you accept Jesus as your personal savior it is kind of like deciding you want to run a marathon, what is the first thing you do? You go buy a pair of shoes. The shoes do not mean you are ready to run a complete marathon, but the first step in a lifelong process. I have been relentlessly pursuing knowledge of God and how he works, preaching and growing for the past 8 years. However, as to my progress in the marathon…I can barely crawl to the mailbox.

I cringe when pastors create this mystical environment behind some moving music and dim lights…God is bigger than this! A relationship with Christ is growing every day. There is a sticky note on my computer that I read every day…it reads "The origin of all Sin is reducing God to something you can understand." You see, churches can be guilty of "packaging" the gospel in a guilt ridden box of "…you are not good enough, work harder…" messages that simply let you leave wondering if you are really saved or not? I still think and act badly, sometimes repressively…I guess I am not really saved? No, not at all! If you freely accept Jesus, his Grace and Mercy save you, not your works. The change that you go through is so incremental (if it is going to be sustainable), you may barely notice it.

Another example of sustainable growth is watching your child grow. I never saw my daughters' growth slowly equal the height of their mother's, but it happened. There is a disease called *osteogenesis imperfecta* that causes the bones to be fragile and easily broken because they grow too fast. That quick growth is unsustainable. Quite the same, Jesus often used examples of botanical growth to demonstrate our growth in Him. From a seed to a tree that bears fruit, it takes time and the growth is mostly unnoticeable, but it is growing…just like your faith.

I was sitting at the breakfast table with our family and explained the three most important things you can work on to ensure you are growing in Christ. Of course the fact we were at breakfast made this lesson stick for all of us, including me! EGG, I said. The constant practice of EGG! Empathy, Graciousness and Gratefulness. These are all emotions that separate you from self. The key to any spiritual growth is separation of self and taking on the feeling of others as more important. This sounds easy, but is contradictory to all that this life externally teaches us.

Empathy is a real key in this equation. I remember hearing about my grandmother having a car accident in Lakeland, Florida, when I was about 16 years old. I spoke to her on the phone and asked her what happened? Her reply I only now truly understand. She said; "I ran a green light". I asked her if she was okay, and she said she was fine just sore from the airbag going off and leaving her with some nasty bruising. I told her how sorry I was, expressing my sympathy, and went on with my day. I really did not think anything more about it; I just went back to what I was doing. About a week or so later we went from our home in Ocoee, Florida, to visit her. When she answered the door I saw the bruising still evident. I was physically moved almost to the point of crying. I was feeling her pain. It went from sympathy to empathy. A part of me actually wanted to hurt hoping that it would somehow relieve her hurt.

I don't remember many times my family went to visit her and my grandfather, (on my mother's side), that she and Bernie were not on the porch reading their Bible. Although I was saved at 16, I had little more than fire insurance. I remember getting hand written letters from her pleading with me to take my relationship with Jesus seriously, and dedicate myself to his service, but I would shrug it off thinking I was okay where I was. She was unarguably one of the most important figures in my spiritual life. I wish I had not waited 20 or more years, and after her death, to take her advice…oh what pain and sorrow I could have avoided.

Back to her comment, "I ran a green light". You might think that that was a falsely humble thing to say, and undoubtedly at the time that probably entered into my mind as one of those "crazy Christian" things to say, but it was not. She truly had been so committed to Jesus that she had no concern for herself and actually felt worse for the guy that ran the red light. I would be willing to bet that she cared more about his possible injuries than hers the entire time of her recovery. She was so practiced in empathy, graciousness and gratefulness that she was almost incapable of thinking of herself. Every time I tell this story I realize how far I have to go. I think of MAYBE being able to crawl to the mailbox and even question that. She was a pillar of faith and trust in Jesus Christ.

A concept that I try to stress with anyone close to me is never think of the word fair. We really don't want "fair". If only from a physical perspective...if fair was instituted there would be a sudden redistribution of wealth throughout the world, and anyone living in the United States would take such a tremendous step back so that their current lives would be unrecognizable. It is a fact that if you live under a bridge in the United States you are in the top 10% of the world as far as wealth, food and healthcare. Do you really want fair? It is only when you embrace this fact that you can ever come close to being grateful in any circumstance. When you are truly grateful for your worst days it will manifest itself in a gracious spirit that has no trouble putting others first. Your humility will be a by-product and not a forced effort. This is truly the essence of sustainable growth.

Happiness and Peace cannot be procured, only earned through self-sacrifice and service to others.

Consumer God!

Ahhh, this is a simple concept that will single-handedly separate you from about 98% of all Christian Churches. What I mean by Consumer God is best explained by understanding the word consumer/ consumerism: a person who purchases goods and services for personal use. In other words, if I do, I should get. A better way of understanding this concept is an example I use in ministry often...If I walk into my favorite grocery store, Kroger's, with a ten dollar bill, I have a reasonable expectation of leaving the store with my favorite smoked cheddar cheese, saltine crackers and a half gallon of skim milk. My reasonable expectation is based on a consumer relationship with Kroger's. If Kroger's quits stocking my favorite smoked cheddar cheese, and I discover Publix now carries it...well, as a consumer, I will then take my consumer relationship to Publix. I will go where my consumer relationships are reasonably beneficial for both parties.

My favorite example of consumer relationships rears its ugly head in 67% of marriages, which end in divorce. We meet, fall in love, have kids, and then…she lost her job and can't carry her financial part…she gains some weight and I lose my physical interest…we grow apart…he starts working late…he does not show the "love" anymore, sex becomes stagnant, etc. You see; these are all because the marriage was based on, or at least a large portion was based on, a consumer relationship. "If I do this…then I should have a reasonable expectation that she does this". This relationship by its very nature is destined to fail with the inevitable changes of any season.

This mentality is simply flawed as it is based on appetite. An appetite involves the satisfying of basic physical needs. If I am hungry I eat. If I decide it is too far to walk, I buy a car. If I want more money, I work harder. If I am tired, I sleep. In the book of I Corinthians Paul said it is better to marry then to burn with lust, thus satisfying a physical appetite.

1 Corinthians 7:8-9
⁸Now to the unmarried and the widows I say: It is good for them to stay unmarried, as I do. ⁹But if they cannot control themselves, they should marry, for better to marry than to burn with passion.

Again, at first glance you might think that Paul was giving his okay to being drawn into a physical/appetite driven existence. In fact what he was saying is that balance would be the only way to adequately keep your prayer and service life alive. He was explaining that not all people can be like him and abstain from the physical desires of a partner. However, again, this is an appetite and left unchecked appetites always grow and take much discipline in order to not be mastered by, but to master. I will write more about this in the chapter "Tea with the Devil".

And yet so many make choices based on social strata. Having three kids I see this relational phenomena often in their choice of friends. They choose friends that they can somehow leverage for social gain or increased popularity. Of course this is a reciprocal process. You see this play out as their friendships are hot and cold and generally short in their life span. I don't know very many people who have best friends in elementary school and go on to have those "best friends" throughout their lives. Often, once the friendship no longer provides a ladder for social influence or gain it is no longer mutual.

Currently, I run a company with about 290 employees. I love each and every one of these employees, some I don't even know. I have an exceptionally close circle of 7 executives. I am not so foolish as to think that at least a portion, hopefully small, of our relationship is based on the consumer model…they work and have a reasonable expectation that I will pay them a very nice salary and sometimes a bonus for above average company profits.

The real rub comes between two words, involvement and commitment. There is an age-old parable that many motivational speakers reference in differentiating these two words: In a bacon and egg breakfast, the chicken was involved however the pig was committed. From a consumer aspect the chicken is a better short-term investment, as you will have a reasonable expectation of continued return. However the investment in the pig requires finality of thought with no return outside the commitment. There is no better representation then the words that came out of Jesus' mouth as he took his last breath on the cross.

John 19:30
When he had received the drink, Jesus said, "It is finished." With that, he bowed his head and gave up his spirit.

What Jesus was saying is really quite simple. It is finished! We no longer need to offer up sin or debt sacrifices for God's approval. Jesus was the final sacrifice, the perfect lamb that history had been waiting for thousands of years and the redemption of our souls if we so choose to accept it. It is really that simple. However the confusion comes with a very simple misdirection of scripture for "consumer" centered needs. There is a scripture that reads; you work out your salvation with fear and trembling... If mismanaged you could (and most churches do) turn this into a physical model: i.e. if you accept Jesus you should join a church, tithe, help others, volunteer etc. These are all extremely important by-products of your new life in Christ, however by-products are different than ingredients. Ingredients are physical; by-products are "of" ingredients.

Let me try to clarify this rather muddy subject. In Timothy Keller's book *Prodigal God*, I remember a story that went something like this:

Jesus was walking with and teaching a small group of 12 disciples when out of nowhere asked everyone to pick up a stone and carry it for him. Naturally Peter picked up a small stone John picked up a large stone and the other apostles picked up rather normal sized stones. Jesus did not explain why he wanted them to pick up a stone but simply went on teaching (to everyone's confusion). At lunch that day Jesus said to the disciples, "take out your stone"…As they did, Jesus turned their stone into bread. John had a bountiful lunch and the other disciples ate reasonably well, while Peter had very little to eat. The next day the intimate group were walking and learning from Jesus when out of nowhere Jesus said, "Pick up a stone for me and carry it". Peter, knowing there were only a couple of hours until lunch he picked up the largest stone he could carry for that amount of time and was pleased with himself. The group approached a creek where Jesus said they would eat. Then Jesus said "everyone take out your stone and throw it in the creek." Peter was tired and frustrated and asked Jesus "why, I am hungry and my stone is huge and will be satisfying?" Jesus replied, "Who are you really carrying the stone for?"

Of course this story is not in the Bible, but a wonderful illustration of ingredients and by-product and more importantly committed, or involved. Peter was learning involvement while Jesus was teaching commitment. Peter had a reasonable expectation based on history that the rock would become bread at lunch, when it was not; his consumer heart was on display.

Proverbs 27:20
"Death and destruction are never satisfied, and neither is the human eye"

I was studying the lives of some really cool historical figures a few years ago. I found a common denominator between a few unlikely characters. Charles Darwin, C.S. Lewis and more. They all believed in God at one time, but lost a family member while they were rather young. They were not prepared for that and decided that God was not fair and was not capable of living up to their consumer concept of a "Good God" and walked away from faith (although C.S. Lewis returned with a proper understanding later).

My company, BCS, Inc., decided to help out a church that had recently bought their own building. I agreed to provide janitorial services free of charge for 18 months, and pass on our pricing for consumable supplies such as toilet paper, hand towels and trash bags. This offer was equivalent to about $450 a month or $8,100. Upon meeting my friend he handed me a book on tithing and how it enables God to bless you *in return*. My heart sank, as this is the polar opposite of how God works. I received the book and placed it in the passenger seat of my car, planning to read it or at least browse through it with an open mind at a later time. We walked the building, and with a very kind heart and sincere appreciation for our offer to help his Church he said: "God is going to bless you for this". All I could think was that this is why I am writing this book!

The premise that financial tithing somehow triggers God's blessings is simply insane to me. Tithing is about sacrifice not money. I know many people that are worth millions that subconsciously think they can tithe their way to heaven without the sacrifice of comfort at all. I personally am aware of a gentleman that supplies 70% of the funding for a prominent TV ministry who is quite content paying as long as it is comfortable. But feeding the hungry or loving someone that really needs it…not going to happen -- that is for people whose time is less valuable.

I was ministering in jail one night with a group of about 14 inmates, and subject of tithing came up. An older gentleman with graying hair and rough graying beard said, "When I got out last time I tried to join a Church and they did not think it was time for me unless I could agree to a monthly tithing amount to prove my commitment". It was all I could do to not to cry in front of all these men. Definitely not the message I had intended to give, but one I had to set straight no matter who I offended.

Hebrews 7:1-4
This Melchizedek was king of Salem and priest of God Most High.
He met Abraham returning from the defeat of the kings and blessed
him, and Abraham gave him a tenth of everything. First, the name
Melchizedek means "king of righteousness"; then also, "king of
Salem" means "king of peace." Without father or mother, without
genealogy, without beginning of days or end of life, resembling the
Son of God, he remains a priest forever.

Most of the pastors that want to promote tithing financially 10% of one's income will undoubtedly use this scripture as a reference. There are three important things to keep in context: 1. Abram was giving the first 10% of plunder gained from caravanning or stealing from neighboring tribes or villages... **not cash!** 2. Most all of the references of giving dealt with land use deals, **not cash!** (I.e. Every 8th year you were to leave your crops for the community.) 3. Abram was before the law was instituted therefore not considered under law or the New Covenant. Nowhere does it mention giving 10% of your annual income to a Church to trust to adequately distribute to those in need.

Before you get too haughty and frustrated…I do believe time, talent and resources is the by-product of a healthy relationship with Jesus Christ, not an ingredient. Very important to be able to make that distinction. I also believe giving to your local church is very important as long as they are using it to grow people in a relationship with Jesus Christ and not growing their building and naming the streets after themselves.

Back to the gentleman with tears in his eyes, after being told it was necessary that he made a commitment of 10% of his income or a financial amount of some sort to become a member. After mentioning the preceding definitions found throughout the bible and bringing tithing into context I asked him a simple question. "Would you prefer me to pay your mortgage and car payment this month while you are in jail, or would you prefer for me to come into this jail, sacrificing time with my family, to tell you that I love you, God loves you and God has an important plan for your life that you simply do not want to miss out on? That God is bigger than your past failures and capable of making your worst pain of defeat and failure become your greatest weapon for your future war against the flesh"? I would not make this up…the man not only began to cry, but two other men (in jail remember...not a place you want to show weakness...) fought back tears as well. It was so clear that he understood...it was so clear that he got that church/God is not a building and a set of arbitrary rules but that indeed God is the manifestation of love.

Again the point of tithing is making it uncomfortable and at a sacrifice. For me...I would love to sit back and simply write a check for 10% and think that was an adequate response. A response for the maker of heaven and earth watching his son beaten (flogging was practically an art to see how badly you could beat a person without them actually dying) within inches of his life only to later be put on a cross to die for my sin...a penalty that I should have to serve. I believe my response should be a bit more than 10% of my financial income...It should be 100% of everything - it should be real commitment.

Romans 5:8
But God demonstrates his own love for us in this: While we were still sinners, Christ died for us.

Every religion in the world says; "if you do this...you should have a reasonable expectation that you can expect that..." Christ following / The Way says: Nothing you can do will ever enable you to be worthy for what has already been done for you. You can't faith your way in, you simply believe that Christ died for your sins and sits at the right hand of the father awaiting you in his time to spend eternity in his presences. At that time all of your questions will be answered and he will reveal himself as who he is...The great "I am"!

Romans 10:9
If you declare with your mouth, "Jesus is Lord," and believe in your heart that God raised him from the dead, you will be saved.

Churches often misguide (I make no apologies for using the word often!) congregations into thinking that tithing or deeds will enable spiritual growth, thus increasing your favor with God, help you have a more meaningful relationship with Christ or the *absolute* worst; if you tithe God will bless you as a result of your tithe. This is simply horribly wrong and a massively unsustainable relational concept when describing how God works through us on this earth as a by-product of our acceptance of his son Jesus / Emmanuelle (God with us). It helps, through guilt, to keep the lights on and to build bigger buildings, but not sustainable. It is the epicenter of consumer God, also currently referred to as prosperity ministry.

God gave his only son so that we would be made righteous and blameless. God owes me nothing more! Jesus laid down his life for me while I was still a sinner and he owes nothing more! Jesus was beaten within inches of his life and then deserted by those he loved to die alone as a murderer or thief would... He owes me NOTHING MORE! If I ever tithe, volunteer or love the unlovable for anything more than my absolute *awe/fear/love* of Jesus -- who was so committed to me that I would have the immeasurable honor to reciprocate that commitment to him -- (pitiful as my reciprocity is), I would reduce my Savior to the status of a grocery store.

Cult vs. Truth

If your basic understanding of sin is Law, you will criticize yourself and others…Sin is breaking God's heart!

Matthew 15:1-7
[1]Then some Pharisees and teachers of the law came to Jesus from Jerusalem and asked, [2] "Why do your disciples break the tradition of the elders? They don't wash their hands before they eat!" [3]Jesus replied, "And why do you break the command of God for the sake of your tradition? [4] For God said, 'Honor your father and mother' and 'anyone who curses their father or mother is to be put to death. [5] But you say that if anyone declares that what might have been used to help their father or mother is 'devoted to God,' [6] they are not to 'honor their father or mother' with it. Thus you nullify the word of God for the sake of your tradition. [7] You hypocrites! Isaiah was right when he prophesied about you

Wow, there is some mostly unknown depth here. It is the absolute best representation of the imbalance of truth and grace. The Pharisees and Sadducee's had created (for the sake of power and control) a "Holy Huddle" that was law driven. They had a private club that enabled them to justify what they wanted as they could legally bend the Law to meet their needs while persecuting those with their free hand.

The Pharisees were experts on the law and believed in a strict adherence to important interpretations of the law as a path to holiness. The **Sadducees**, who were a priestly class, focused on the Temple as the path to holiness.

Notice in verse 2 the Pharisees are calling out Jesus and his disciples for not washing before they eat, which was (Andy Stanley term here) guardrail commandment to prevent the breaking of the actual 10 major commandments. [Context break here: 613 Mitzvot's/Levitical commandments/laws, and 10 major, obviously known as the 10 commandments. Jesus is basically saying…you want to call me out for speeding while you commit murder? Really?]

Ephesians 6:2-3
² "Honor your father and mother" which is the first commandment with a promise ³ "so that it may go well with you and that you may enjoy long life on the earth."

You see, the Pharisees had created this private country club for "do gooders" (at least outside perception) while they insulated themselves with power, control and all the trappings that this provided while neglecting the commandment of taking care of their parents. "You hypocrites" They could have been legally stoned to death for breaking this commandment.

Grace; without it we are dead in our sin, or left to justify ourselves by works, which will never be enough (and simple death by paper cuts)…

Ephesians 2:2-10
²As for you, you were dead in your transgressions and sins, in which you used to live when you followed the ways of this world and of the ruler of the kingdom of the air, the spirit who is now at

work in those who are disobedient. [3] All of us also lived among them at one time, gratifying the cravings of our flesh and following its desires and thoughts. Like the rest, we were by nature deserving of wrath. [4] But because of his great love for us, God, who is rich in mercy, [5] made us alive with Christ even when we were dead in transgressions—it is by grace you have been saved. [6] And God raised us up with Christ and seated us with him in the heavenly realms in Christ Jesus, [7] in order that in the coming ages he might show the incomparable riches of his grace, expressed in his kindness to us in Christ Jesus. [8] For it is by grace you have been saved, through faith - and this is not from yourselves, it is the gift of God - [9] not by works, so that no one can boast. [10] For we are God's handiwork, created in Christ Jesus to do good works, which God prepared in advance for us to do.

Here is what most churches don't really want you to know: You don't need to go to church to go to heaven (although you are foolish not to); you don't necessarily need to be good to go to heaven, who is? You need to be forgiven! Which only comes through the grace of Jesus Christ who died to carry our sin debt. He took on our punishment in order to cover us in Grace if we so choose to make him our Savior and accept the free gift of eternal life through his Grace.

John 3:16
For God so loved the world that he gave his one and only Son, that whoever believes in him shall not perish but have eternal life.

I would have to say this is pretty clear!

This is the really cool part; I bet you did not know? Do you know what separates Christianity from every other religion in history? Every religion in history says, goodness, moral teaching and to do lists and maybe you will get in…(to paradise). Christianity says: that's not nearly enough! A savior is the only way you can get in (to heaven).

I recently read a book by Andy Stanley that was titled *How Good is Good Enough*? It was a tremendously insightful book about Christianity as it compares to all other religions. The bottom line of the book is that good people don't go to heaven, forgiven people go to heaven. *That is Grace!* Man, I don't want what I deserve on my most charitable day. I want Grace brother, because my best day does not deserve the presence of Jesus and my father God!

Ok, you knew this was coming… the rub!

Jude 1:3-4
³ Dear friends, although I was very eager to write to you about the salvation we share, I felt compelled to write and urge you to contend for the faith that was once for all entrusted to God's holy people. ⁴ For certain individuals whose condemnation was written about long ago have secretly slipped in among you. They are ungodly people, who pervert the grace of our God into a license for immorality and deny Jesus Christ our only Sovereign and Lord.

1 Corinthians 6:12
"I have the right to do anything," you say—but not everything is beneficial. "I have the right to do anything"—but I will not be mastered by anything.

You are free through the death and resurrection, but if you truly understand the cost of this freedom, it will change everything you do—and think.

This is the best example I can come up with: My neighbor just found out that I have been diagnosed with a terminal heart condition and have 3 months to live, unless I get a transplant. They do not know much about my family, and I don't know much about theirs. I do know their kids have graduated college and are married starting their own families. They know I have three young children and see me playing outside with them routinely, but that is about the extent of the relationship. I got a call from my Doctor; she said that my neighbor said that he wanted to give me his heart so that I could continue to be a father to my children. He said that he had already had that time with his kids and that time with kids when they're young was so important that he was willing to die for me, barely knowing me, then to know that he could have prevented my death and missing that experience. Now, I have a question... Do you take the heart say thank you, try to work to be a better person and continue on with your life; or would you take an interest in getting to know more about this man who laid down his life for you? Would you take care of his widowed wife and children? Would it change everything about how you live? Don't know?

You see the person that can take it without responsibility, never really got it. Accepting Jesus will get you into heaven, but if you want peace, joy, love and understanding… you will strive to get to know the man who gave it all for you. You can accept the gift, but the joy is understanding and learning to <u>act like the giver</u>.

Don't get me wrong here…Law is important, but absent of an equal measure of grace is death. I was becoming disgusted with Law heavy Christian school/jail my children were going to at the time. I used the following example to teach my children that God does not give us rules to keep us from having fun; he gives us rules to keep us from getting hurt!

We got a new dog, a boxer, a few years ago, and Rebecca decided to name him Chaz. Turns out...that was a very appropriate name. "Chaz the Spaz"! Shortly after he was two years old, he found an open garage door and was off to explore all he had seen from only the window until then. From the window it looked harmless and fun. Well, he got into the street, running from me frantically trying to catch him. Right before my eyes he got hit by a mini-van and literally went flying 20 feet in the air. Immediately I went to my knees and cried. Before I could muster the strength to go pick him up I looked up and he struggled to walk back to me and sit right in front of me as if to say, "Dad, this really hurts and it is my fault, I am sorry". I cannot make this up. After thoroughly checking him out (no broken bones etc.), I put him on our bed and cared for him for the next three days, not sure if he was going to make it or not. He did! After about a week or so he got back to normal.

I sat my kids down and posed this question: If I sat Chaz down and asked him if he would like a fence in the backyard to protect him from danger, what do you think he would say? They replied, he would say I promise I will stay within the boundaries. Of course, but the boundaries expand over time as curiosity does. Before you realize it, you are in the road. This is what the law is for; this is what rules are for at their core.

Often you see churches creating this environment of guilt and fear in order to keep congregations in line. "If you are a sinner, you are going to Hell." "If you drink, fart, burp, curse etc., you are going to Hell." In other words, "Fear is the bait to all cages." Often I hear "Christians" loosely quote 1 Corinthians 6 (always out of context or complete ignorance) to justify their judging of peoples' sins. Shortly before quoted 1 Corinthians 6:12 you find this:

1 Corinthians 6:9-11
⁹ Or do you not know that the unrighteous will not inherit the kingdom of God? Do not be deceived: neither the sexually immoral, nor idolaters, nor adulterers, nor men who practice homosexuality, ¹⁰ nor thieves, nor the greedy, nor drunkards, nor revilers, nor swindlers will inherit the kingdom of God. ¹¹ And such were some of you. But you were washed, you were sanctified, you were justified in the name of the Lord Jesus Christ and by the Spirit of our God.

At first glance you see the fire and brimstone waiting to give birth in the closest Baptist congregation. The first thing you will do, by our sinful nature, is start checking off the things that you don't do on the list, and look for someone that is on the list! Hold on; let's examine neighbors of drunkard, sexually immoral, thieves and homosexual…How about greedy, which is immense coveting? How about swindler, which is someone who conducts himself or herself in a selfish manner for personal gain? *Ouch!* How about revilers/slanderers, which is basically talking badly behind someone's back? I am sure you are like me, and innocent of all of those, but if not…

That is why we need a savior who died to forgive us. Not to enable us to continue to sin, but to be there on bended knees waiting for us to return and nurse us back to health. That is Grace.

Anytime you see an imbalance with a grace heavy church, sin and acceptance of it will be loud and out of control. Anytime you see an imbalance of Law in a church you will have the same sin, but they will add lying about it and hiding in the closet, and sure they are capable of judging when someone else's closet door becomes ajar. These are cults, not churches.

If your basic understanding of sin is Law, you will criticize yourself and others…Sin is breaking God's heart!

Law is important but only when you receive the free gift of balance, which is Grace!

$$(G+M) + (S+V) = R2$$

This is one of my favorite lessons of all time. I remember giving a leadership training for executives meeting a few years ago and started it with this formula. I prefaced the meeting by offering a financial reward to anyone who could solve it. I posted it in large letters on four walls in our conference room. The clues went like this: 1. We all need it... 2. We will spend our lives trying to achieve it... 3. Christ died to give it to us... 4. Your whole life is connected to it...

It is the formula to relationships *exponentialized*. (Grace + Mercy) + (Submission + Vulnerability) = Relationships Squared. Even better explained as truly unconditional love.

Grace, or, giving what is undeserved: If someone runs their car into your front yard fence, you meet them and decide that you will pay for the repair cost instead of having them pay for the damage they caused. Mercy, or withholding from someone what they deserve. The emotion of mercy precedes the ability to extend grace. Forgiveness on an unconditional basis is a good way of looking at these two. You can extend grace but still emotionally hold the person hostage. In your heart you can forgive but still hold a grudge. I often say, "forgiveness pays the debt, everything else pays interest". Sometimes we extend grace for the external sake of what people will say of us, but we extend mercy for what we think God will think of us.

Practicing grace and mercy with people, friends and foes, starts with a complete understanding that only God gives and takes away.

1 Corinthians 10:26
"The earth is the Lord's, and everything in it."

Ephesians 4:32
Be kind and compassionate to one another, forgiving each other, just as in Christ God forgave you.

Undoubtedly I see this dichotomy in Christians primarily. I often see people with the ability (me included) forgiving on the outside but holding hostage the need to see justice. There is a great saying, "Justice for all and mercy for me".

In order to forgive but hold hostage, you have to start with one simple fact, you are the God and not the God whose story spans all of history. You have to either hold your opinion in such high regard that you have become the person God has put on this earth to do His bidding…or you have reduced God to something so simple that you have not only figured it out, but now believe you really know what right and wrong are and have the confidence to distribute fair and righteous judgment. No middle ground here! Again, **no middle ground!** If your physical is not in line with your heart it is for everyone but God!

If you currently live on earth you will fight this battle for the entirety of your life. However, if you chose not to fight and simply accept "this is the way I was made" you chose to lose the battle and hand yourself over, and will do the same to the next earthly principal that has not given God enough credit to help you fight.

1 Peter 2:11
Dear friends, I urge you, as foreigners and exiles, to abstain from sinful desires, which wage war against your soul.

As if the preceding is not hard enough…Now we get to the hard part: Submission and Vulnerability!

Matthew 7:13-14
[13] "Enter through the narrow gate. For wide is the gate and broad is the road that leads to destruction, and many enter through it. [14] But small is the gate and narrow the road that leads to life, and only a few find it.

At first glance this verse seems like a perpetual donning of a straightjacket. In fact, many theologies package the walk with Christ as a list of do's and do not's. In fact, nothing could be further from the truth. I remember hearing the following story:

If you walk to and from school every day for 4 years, and right before you get to school there is a long fence about 8 feet high. The last day of school on your way you notice a hole just above eyesight. You are curious? On the way home you notice that someone put a note below the hole that reads, "Under no circumstances should you look into this hole". What are you going to want to do? Yes, the ugliness of the 'to do' list revealed! You have to understand God knows us and our relentless opposition to lists of to do's and not to do's. In the chapter "The Ten Commandments," I will go into the math of this disease.

So how do I grow in Christ with this monkey on my back for opposing all to do lists (a misunderstanding of The Ten Commandments in the primary)?

Become "narrow"!

The phrase "narrow is the gate" is fairly easy to understand. A narrow gate is harder to pass through than one that is wide, and only a few people can go through a narrow gate at once. In saying, "difficult is the way which leads to life," Jesus was explaining how hard being a Christian really is.

"Narrow" is from the Greek word thlibo, which means: "To press (as grapes), press hard upon; a compressed way; narrow straitened, contracted" (New Testament Greek Lexicon, www.bibletstudytools.com). The lexicon adds that the word can be used metaphorically to mean, "trouble, afflict, and distress." If Jesus wanted to draw people to follow him, why did he tell prospective disciples that doing so would bring them grief?

This really speaks to the previous chapter concerning Consumer God and commitment vs. involvement. Jesus was truly giving the essence of what following would be...difficult. So many times I see professing Christians run to physical remedies for spiritual issues. In essence we run to our "reliable and consolably Gods" instead of totally submitting to our professed belief that he can and will hold us when we are at our weakest.

2 Corinthians 12:9
⁹ But he said to me, "My grace is sufficient for you, for my power is made perfect in weakness." Therefore I will boast all the more gladly about my weaknesses, so that Christ's power may rest on me.

I often analyze myself, and my default positions, and the biggest tell-tale sign of my current spiritual condition is where I run when the crap is hitting the fan. Where do you run? Most of us run to those who we assume will stay on our side, and tell us what we want to hear. Unfortunately, this is truly submitting and being vulnerable to a false God. It is comfortable, and for the most part predictable. It is not narrow! It is wide!

Is it total acceptance of "…your will be done on earth as it is in heaven"? This simply means, I admit that I have no control, and I lay down what little I thought I had. It means, even though I don't understand your ways, I submit my life to them and trust your story is bigger than my life and illusion of control of it.

What Jesus was saying is that unless you can totally submit to his story, you will never see it on earth or in heaven. You have to lay your life down and become as vulnerable as a child.

Matthew 18:3
And he said: "Truly I tell you, unless you change and become like

83

little children, you will never enter the kingdom of heaven.

Think about the most important relationships in your life. Do you have anything you are holding back? If you are truly honest with yourself, your earthly relationships always have a certain "thing" that has been purposely omitted due to the fear of "what they would think if they knew".

Men especially have a problem with vulnerability. Men are taught at an early age that crying is for girls. We are told to be tough, and short of that is weakness. This really goes against what Jesus was telling us we needed in order to have real relationships. We need to be weak in ourselves in order to be strong in him. We need to be reliant on him in order to deal with this earth. We need to be narrow, compressed, and puddled on the ground in order to truly be in relationship with him. We need to be vulnerable and submitted in order to have *exponientialized* relationships with anyone.

I promise you that if you practice this formula with your closest friends you will either become closer then you ever knew you could be or find yourself purging those friends that are not equally yoked with you. Either outcome is one HUGE step towards a more meaningful relationship with your creator.

2 Corinthians 6:14
[14] Be ye not unequally yoked together with unbelievers: for what fellowship hath righteousness with unrighteousness? And what communion hath light with darkness?

Tea with the Devil

"Don't get hit by life's bus chasing your P.I.G.S!"

This is one of my favorite sayings. As with many quotes there is a TON of depth that lurks beneath the obvious. Let me first define P.I.G.S – Problematic, Immediate, Gratifiers. It is not if your life gets dismantled by chasing immediate gratification desires, it is when. There is no way to avoid the eventual and pending "head in hands" moment by not recognizing this simple concept. "How did I get here?"

As I tried to fully explain to my children the importance of not lying, cheating and stealing, I came up with this analogy. P.I.G.S are essentially anything that leverages future for current. I told my kids one day that there are three things that are like having tea with the Devil: 1. Short cuts 2. Short term gains (e.g. lottery) 3. Anything immediately gratifying (sex, drugs and rock and roll).

I say this because they all take on the guise of "it's not that bad", "it's not going to kill me" or "only this one time". I call this concept "Tea with the Devil". I used the analogy of meeting with the Devil over something as innocuous as tea. At first glance it just seems like tea, nothing big or life changing. A simple meet and greet. Before you realize it you're meeting once a week and find yourself saying…"He is really not that bad of a guy". Another look might be a moderate bending of rules, but not outright breaking them. A simple omission of facts, but not lying. Simply finding some money on the floor by a cashier but not stealing it. Before you realize it, the slow fade has enabled you to do things you never would have done just a few short years earlier. You have become smitten by the Devil without even knowing it.

In a previous chapter I wrote about PACC (Power, Acceptance, Control and Comfort). If in your life you see a constant in any of these categories…

Would you like milk or sugar with your tea?

Sidetrack…I need to explain something called "The Principle of Pathway". What this means is that pathway equals destination not intention. Have you ever heard the bible verse "the road to hell is paved with good intentions"? Probably not, because it's not in there, but it should be… Think about it--it does not matter how bad you want to go to Florida, but if you're heading North on 75, you won't get there. You might have packed your bathing suits, towels, sunscreen and beach chairs… But you will not find that Florida beach you so want to see.

Especially in the United States, where everything is a button away, we are drawn to immediate gratification. Immediate satisfaction should be called pathway to terminal destruction. Don't get me wrong, I believe, like many things, certain luxuries of immediate satisfaction are a good thing. However, when a good thing becomes an ultimate thing you have the primary definition of addiction. This is what I refer to as the slow fade.

C.S Lewis, from the Screwtape Letters:

"Indeed the safest road to Hell is the gradual one--the gentle slope, soft underfoot, without sudden turnings, without milestones, without sign posts, your affectionate uncle, Screwtape."

You have to realize first that immediate is *never* really immediate in its real finality sense of the word. Immediate satisfaction things have long term effects on your heart and your environmental predispositions. It slowly trains your brain that all things should have immediate remedies, results and worst of all, conclusions.

My daughter is now 17 and dating a fine young man. I like to think that I have a very open relationship with her, and take the trust she has in my advice very seriously. She has been dating him for almost a year. As a father of an exceptionally beautiful girl (inside and out), I am naturally hyper concerned with her interaction with boys. I explained that boys are generally over sexually curious during these adolescent years and even into their young adult years. I explained, the best that I could, the massive importance of setting parameters of what she will and will not do before marriage. I told her of the many things and situations that will arise that will push her ability to hold to those standards. I told her that she cannot imagine the temptation and difficulties of staying true to her beliefs and morals, especially in her coming college years.

Most recently I recall a conversation about kissing. I asked her a few months ago if they had kissed. She said no. I asked her if they were talking about it. She said yes. I then left the conversation alone. Well, a couple of months later, I asked the question again. I asked her how she felt when they kissed. Was she nervous? Did she feel cold inside? Etc....I left the conversation alone for a while. Of course, I had to bring up again...I am a DAD! I asked her if they kiss every time they see each other now. She said yes. So I explained this is the slow fade in process. I don't mean this as a bad thing, just as a fact of energy in motion. I asked her to remember the first kiss, and how long they had talked about it and how nervous she was the first time and maybe the next two or three. Then I asked her to explain why it is not so scary anymore. Of course she got it right away. The slow fade is always at work, but never noticeable at ground level. What was scary is now normal, what was unthinkable is now daily.

Virtually every story I hear young men in jail talk to me about always ends in "…how did I get from there to here"? Slow Fade! Many years of the slow fade principle working unseen or noticed makes a person slowly move their moral compass until it is unrecognizable and primarily responsible for the following years of despair, regret and heart damage.

So, how do I "undo" the damage I have incurred by not being aware of this slow fade energy I have been engulfed in my entire life? Well, that is easier said than done. It all hinges on a single word, "Repent". One of the words that for as long as I have gone to church, I have been spiritually dismantled by the misrepresentation of this word.

Peter was addressing a crowd after many of them had finally realized that they had crucified their savior. Jesus had been put on a cross and appeared resurrected, and the realization of the unimaginable guilt led to this exchange:

Acts 2:37-38

When the people heard this, they were cut to the heart and said to Peter and the other apostles, "Brothers, what shall we do? "Peter replied, "Repent and be baptized, every one of you, in the name of Jesus Christ for the forgiveness of your sins. And you will receive the gift of the Holy Spirit.

The word for repent in Greek is "metanoia". Metenoia means to change your mind. Every time I have heard these verses preached, I have been dismantled mentally by the interpretation of the word "repent". Most, and I mean *most*, pastors insist that repenting from past sinful behavior happens the minute you accept Christ as your savior. Upon that acceptance you don't sin anymore. In other words, and I have heard this preached, if you sin again then your salvation is not real or at the very least in jeopardy. *Wrong*! When you repent, you change the way you are looking at things. When I got saved and decided to repent, I decided to make my life accountable to God and his gift and not to others and myself. The changes in my life could very well be unrecognizable to most people that know me, but to me…

93

Unmistakable. I don't have to make excuses for my behavior I have to make apologies. I don't justify my sinful desires, I fight them day-by-day. In short, God's presence has replaced mine. The Holy Spirit has replaced my subconscious. I simply can no longer run or cover up the fact that that Truth is written on my heart, and I will no longer try to cover it up to "get along" in this world. I will face the fact that I am a broken sinner incapable of ever being worth what God did for me through his Son. But the fact that he loves me anyway, will not let me remain the same as I was yesterday. I want to be better for him, and then better for my children and all who know me. That is repentance!

You have to see, that repentance is a slow fade in the opposite direction. As in many cases in life, simply turning the car around is the best way to find your way back home. I can want to become a new creation in Christ (intention) or I can turn my car around (pathway) and become a new creation in Christ. We don't destroy our hearts quickly, and we certainly won't clean them quickly, but with repentance and prayer you can correct your pathway and hence find your intended destination.

One last story that happened last week. I got a call from a BIC (brother in Christ), Mark. Mark is one of my closest and dearest friends. He was audibly upset at something his son did, accidentally. His son, 7 years old, was on the computer studying for something for school and got sidetracked and ended up on an inappropriate internet site. He and his wife are mortified and not quite sure what to do as punishment. He told me that Charlie was very upset at what he had seen. He also told me that he had been warned several times before of how quickly you can click on a bad link and all of the sudden… you are looking at something that you should not be. In a much longer conversation I explained to Mark that God has designed this earth's existence so simply (not simplistic mind you) that he has built into it consequences of bad or sinful behavior. I told him that in my house, some of the worst things my kids have done resulted in the least punishment. You see, the consequences of what Charlie saw are far more punishment then what they could do as parents. Sometimes pointing to the fact that we are a creation of God's with God's purposes meant to be pursued is the best lesson we can learn. Sometimes we have to get off the path in order to realize how much safer it really is.

You can never "un-see" what you have seen, you can never "un-speak" what you have spoken and you can never "un-hear" what you have heard. What you see, what you speak and what you hear are who you are. Sometimes we need those awful times to remind us we need to repent and turn the car around. You won't get there overnight, but at least you know when you wake up, and pray, and yes, repent…you are heading in the right direction. This is a lifelong marathon, not a sprint race. As long as sin exists, you will be drawn to it. Rejoice when your pathway enables you to drive by it, and repent when you find yourself in the middle of it.

Romans 5:1-11
[1] Therefore, since we have been justified through faith, we have peace with God through our Lord Jesus Christ, [2] through whom we have gained access by faith into this grace in which we now stand. And we boast in the hope of the glory of God. [3] Not only so, but we also glory in our sufferings, because we know that suffering produces perseverance; [4] perseverance, character; and character, hope. [5] And hope does not put us to shame, because God's love has

been poured out into our hearts through the Holy Spirit, who has been given to us. [6] You see, at just the right time, when we were still powerless, Christ died for the ungodly. [7] Very rarely will anyone die for a righteous person, though for a good person someone might possibly dare to die. [8] But God demonstrates his own love for us in this: While we were still sinners, Christ died for us. [9] Since we have now been justified by his blood, how much more shall we be saved from God's wrath through him! [10] For if, while we were God's enemies, we were reconciled to him through the death of his Son, how much more, having been reconciled, shall we be saved through his life! [11] Not only is this so, but we also boast in God through our Lord Jesus Christ, through whom we have now received reconciliation.

The Ten Commandments

In the front of my bible there are a couple of sticky notes. One note reads, "1. Assume what you are reading is not teaching you what you think, 2. I will misunderstand due to my cultural blinders, 3. Remove your cultural, historical and personal predispositions."

Hebrew writing deals with the spirit of the law vs. the law. Both are important, but the narrative supersedes the dissection of the text. Most of the Old Testament was handed down through oral tradition. Therefore it is vital to understand their methods of communication in order to find the richness of the Old Testament.

Again referencing the 3-point notes in my bible, the first thing I want to note is the cultural bias we have to first address. Often in leadership books and conferences I see the same communication breakdown experiment used. I tell you something, you tell the person next to you, and they tell the person next to them, and over a period of time the story changes dramatically. This is our historical and cultural blinder. The fact is that in the B.C centuries leading up to the writing down of the book of Isaiah and several other Torah books, they, as a culture were far better at communicating verbally accurately through generations. In fact, it was as a group the message was communicated and corroborated in order to ensure accuracy through the years.

The best proof of this is the historical accuracy of Isaiah 53 that was proven by the finding of the Dead Sea Scrolls in Qumran in around 1947. Of all the text that was discovered, Isaiah 53 (written in circa 100 B.C.) was found almost completely intact and it was virtually 100% consistent with the writings that were in question written in 1100 AD, of which King James's translators used to pen the King James Bible. Obviously, this translation was a copy of a copy of a copy, but none the less 100% accurate, over 1700 years of oral progression and then to writing progression.

One important thing to understand about the Hebrew narrative is lists. How and why they used lists to make emotional points later translated to text, which in those days was not nearly as easy as we do today. Less words and less inferences as you can imagine, especially in the western world. Lists act as a type of bookends. The substance between the first and last simply don't stand up without the first and last on that list. This is massively important as it relates to the most famous list of all time (and my favorite, which this book is based on). The Ten Commandments:

1. You shall have no other gods but me
2. You shall not make unto you and graven images
3. You shall not take the name of the Lord your God in vain
4. You shall remember the Sabbath and keep it holy
5. Honor your mother and father
6. You shall not murder
7. You shall not commit adultery
8. You shall not steal
9. You shall not bear false witness
10. You shall not covet anything that belongs to your neighbor

So, how do I read this? Let's take the first commandment; "Have no gods before me!" I could write, and hope to, a complete book on what 'having Gods' means to us in the western world. However, I will keep this simple (and above all accurate) and clear. This most importantly tells us that we are dealing with an almighty monotheistic relationship. There are no more idols, statues, images, etc…One God who is omnipotent! This is a heart issue. If you cannot center your existence on the core belief that there is only one God then nothing else in the list is relevant or applicable in the setting it was intended, spiritually. Now the last, "Don't covet anything that belongs to your neighbor". I have translated this to our way of thinking in this; stop wanting more than you have, and be gracious with your lot knowing full well you don't deserve what you have, let alone the things you set your eyes on. The heart does not desire what the eye does not see.

The simplest way of understanding this is if you picture a cart full of boxes. Imagine the boxes represent the commandments. If you have no wheels the cart goes no place! It starts and ends with its ability to facilitate spiritual movement. One God and a sense of total submission to one's lot. Total heart/spiritual conditions. The others are physical issues.

Once I was asked about the fifth commandment. The gentleman said, "The fifth commandment seems like it is more spiritual than physical". Again, at first glance it does. However that is our cultural blinder again. Honor your mother and father was not a commandment to feel good about them, it was more akin to agape love for them. The relationship should be of total obedience and submission. I read one time it was the practice of submission physically so that you could be eligible to the submission spiritually to God. How can you submit to someone you can't see if you can't submit to someone you can?

Simple, but far from simplistic. Where our heart is, is where our path will lead.

There is an awesome, and I mean awesome, narrative in Luke where Jesus is being tested by these leaders in the law… (physical law of course as he reveals).

Luke 10:25-37
[25] On one occasion an expert in the law stood up to test Jesus. "Teacher," he asked, "what must I do to inherit eternal life?" [26] "What is written in the Law?" he replied. "How do you read it?" [27] He answered, "'Love the Lord your God with all your heart

and with all your soul and with all your strength and with all your mind; and, 'Love your neighbor as yourself.'" ²⁸ "You have answered correctly," Jesus replied. "Do this and you will live." ²⁹ But he wanted to justify himself, so he asked Jesus, "And who is my neighbor?" ³⁰ In reply Jesus said: "A man was going down from Jerusalem to Jericho, when he was attacked by robbers. They stripped him of his clothes, beat him and went away, leaving him half dead. ³¹ A priest happened to be going down the same road, and when he saw the man, he passed by on the other side. ³² So too, a Levite, when he came to the place and saw him, passed by on the other side. ³³ But a Samaritan, as he traveled, came where the man was; and when he saw him, he took pity on him. ³⁴ He went to him and bandaged his wounds, pouring on oil and wine. Then he put the man on his own donkey, brought him to an inn and took care of him. ³⁵ The next day he took out two denarii[e] and gave them to the innkeeper. 'Look after him,' he said, 'and when I return, I will reimburse you for any extra expense you may have.' ³⁶ "Which of these three do you think was a neighbor to the man who fell into the hands of robbers?" ³⁷ The expert in the law replied, "The one who had mercy on him." Jesus told him, "Go and do likewise."

Remember the people Jesus was talking to would have been experts in the Torah, or first 5 books of our current Bible. He looks them in the face and basically says; "God is first, others are second", if you cannot put this into action then you will simply never get it! They were so busy competing for authoritative positions, that promoting and caring for one another became history. Physical behavior superseded Spiritual nurturing... they were dead and knew it!

Jesus uses the character of a Samaritan to hammer his point home. The Samaritans were a kind of cross breed culture. Both the Greeks and the Jews considered them an inferior tribe. Jesus basically says, your heart determines your value in the kingdom. If you think your race determines your value...*wrong*! The Samaritan man not only helped him out of the ditch after being beaten, but he also assisted financially by paying the innkeeper for the time that the man needed to recover. He sacrificed to make sure it would take root...*heart*!

I don't want to be accused of reductionism here, but what does this say? Keep the honor and awe of God first and foremost in your mind in all things you say and do, and Love your neighbor as yourself. Remember, you can forgive yourself of just about anything, how about others? Most of us "mere humanoids" have no trouble holding others to behavior accountability standards that we could not keep on our *best* day! Don't believe me? How about this… What if you had a voice recorder around your neck, and every time you passed judgment on someone as to what they should or should not do, the record button was pushed? How about thinking about your last time driving in rush hour traffic and someone cut in on you without a turn signal? *Record*! How about that time when the shopping cart was not returned properly and scratched your car? *Record*! How about when you hear someone say you said something that you did not? *Record*! Get my point? You have done most things that infuriate you when other people do the same. Simple term for this is "…being your own God". If you are God, well you don't need Him.

What you think you deserve will have everything to do about what you think you want. Someday I hope my default position is nothing, because that is the gateway to true Peace, Joy and Love!

L.I.F. 4:23

Well, if you have read this book and find yourself here; you are probably wondering what the heck does L.I.F mean, yes? Life Is Fun! Life Is Fun- provided you guard your heart. The simple maintenance of your heart will have everything to do with how and what you fully enjoy in this life and in heaven.

John 10:10
The thief only comes to steal, kill, and destroy. I came that they may have life, and may have it abundantly.

Critical life circumstances reveal default positions. Default positions reveal heart conditions… Where is your heart? Where do you run when the crap is hitting the fan?

Proverbs 27: 19:20
As water reflects the face, so one's life reflects the heart. Death and Destruction are never satisfied, and neither are human eyes.

Now for the entire purpose of this book!

Proverbs 4:20-23
[20] My son, pay attention to what I say; turn your ear to my words.
[21] Do not let them out of your sight, keep them within your heart;
[22] for they are life to those who find them and health to one's whole
body. [23] Above all else, guard your heart…

This is *everything*! Solomon is considered the wisest man to ever live. I will spare the history lesson and quote the Bible:

1 Kings 3:1-28
[3]Solomon made an alliance with Pharaoh King of Egypt and married his daughter. He brought her to the City of David until he finished building his palace and the temple of the Lord, and the wall around Jerusalem. [2] The people, however, were still sacrificing at the high places, because a temple had not yet been built for the Name of the Lord. [3] Solomon showed his love for the Lord by walking according to the instructions given him by his father David, except that he offered sacrifices and burned incense

on the high places. ⁴ The king went to Gibeon to offer sacrifices, for that was the most important high place, and Solomon offered a thousand burnt offerings on that altar. ⁵ At Gibeon the Lord appeared to Solomon during the night in a dream, and God said, 'Ask for whatever you want me to give you.' ⁶ Solomon answered, 'you have shown great kindness to your servant, my father David, because he was faithful to you and righteous and upright in heart. You have continued this great kindness to him and have given him a son to sit on his throne this very day. ⁷ 'Now, Lord my God, you have made your servant king in place of my father David. But I am only a little child and do not know how to carry out my duties. ⁸ Your servant is here among the people you have chosen, a great people, too numerous to count or number. ⁹ So give your servant a discerning heart to govern your people and to distinguish between right and wrong. For who is able to govern this great people of yours?' ¹⁰ The Lord was pleased that Solomon had asked for this. ¹¹ So God said to him, 'Since you have asked for this and not for long life or wealth for yourself, nor have asked for the death of your enemies but for discernment in administering justice, ¹² I will do what you have asked. I will give you a wise and discerning heart, so that there will never have been anyone like you, nor will there ever be. ¹³ Moreover, I will give you what you have not asked for – both wealth and honor – so that in your lifetime you will have no equal among kings. ¹⁴ And if you walk in obedience to me and keep my decrees and commands as David your father did, I will give you a long life.' ¹⁵ Then Solomon awoke – and he realized it had been a dream. He returned to Jerusalem, stood before the ark of the Lord's covenant and sacrificed burnt offerings and fellowship offerings. Then he gave a feast for all his court. A wise ruling. ¹⁶ Now two prostitutes came to the king and stood before him. ¹⁷ One of them said, 'Pardon me, my lord. This woman and I live in the same house. I had a baby while she was there with me. ¹⁸ The third day after my child was born, this woman also had a baby. We were alone; there was no one in the house but the two of us. ¹⁹ 'During the night this woman's son died because she lay on him. ²⁰ So she got up in the middle of the night and took my son from my side while I your servant was asleep. She put him by her breast and put her dead son by my breast. ²¹ The next morning, I got up to nurse my son – and he was dead! But when I looked at him closely in the morning light, I saw that it wasn't the son I had borne.' ²² The other woman said, 'No! The living one is my son; the dead one is yours.' But the first one insisted, 'No! The dead one is

yours; the living one is mine.' And so they argued before the king.
²³ The king said, 'This one says, "My son is alive and your son is dead," while that one says, "No! Your son is dead and mine is alive."' ²⁴ Then the king said, 'Bring me a sword.' So they brought a sword for the king. ²⁵ He then gave an order: 'Cut the living child in two and give half to one and half to the other.' ²⁶ The woman whose son was alive was deeply moved out of love for her son and said to the king, 'Please, my lord, give her the living baby! Don't kill him!' But the other said, 'Neither I nor you shall have him. Cut him in two!' ²⁷ Then the king gave his ruling: 'Give the living baby to the first woman. Do not kill him; she is his mother.' ²⁸ When all Israel heard the verdict the king had given, they held the king in awe, because they saw that he had wisdom from God to administer justice.

This is the best snap shot of Solomon. It gives you a great insight into his rise and most of all the humble and selfless nature of his request from God.

Back to Proverbs 4:20-23. Notice how he draws you in…As if to say; "…listen, no really listen, this is big, come be still and let this sink in, no really let this sink in".

1. My son, pay attention to what I say
2. Do not let them out of your sight
3. Keep them within your heart
4. They are life to those who find them
5. They are health to one's *whole* body
6. Guard your heart!

I used to have three monkey candleholders on my desk to remind me of this. The three wise monkeys are a pictorial maxim. Together they embody the proverbial principle "see no evil, hear no evil, speak no evil". The three monkeys are Mizaru, covering his eyes, who sees no evil; Kikazaru, covering his ears, who hears no evil; and Iwazaru, covering his mouth, who speaks no evil.

Your eyes, ears and what you speak are like a little seeding factory. What you put into them will have everything to do with your heart condition. Scientists have linked murderous video games to several school shootings. This example is too dramatic for what I'm trying to explain, but it does show the process of desensitization is slow and barely noticeable until it has infected your *whole* body.

I was in the car one day with a guy I work with, Patrick, and he asked me; "Is Christian music all you listen to anymore?" I replied, "Yes, I am not ready for the other music yet". Keep in mind, I play guitar and drums and love music, especially Stevie Ray Vaughn, Led Zeppelin and many other hard rock and blues artist. This was quite the sabbatical for me. However, as I understand Proverbs 4:23, this was essential at the time for my spiritual growth. I have since introduced mild levels of some of that secular music, but as I type I have the Hillsong United iTunes playing.

In addition, for several years I refused to watch a rated R movie. I have seen a few in the last few years, but always feel a little dirty after seeing things that I did not necessarily want to see. I am fully aware that I have by choice let bad seeds into my heart, and then have an uphill battle of squashing them out.

Words have power brother, words have power!

Proverbs 18:20-21
20 From the fruit of their mouth a person's stomach is filled; with the harvest of their lips they are satisfied. 21 The tongue has the power of life and death, and those who love it will eat its fruit.

The condition of your heart is the limitations of your ability to speak life into people. Most of us are so worried about the comparison game, or the fair game that we approach most conversations with little thought of our responsibility to leave that person with the seed of love. How often do you have a conversation (without selfish gain) with someone waiting for the opportunity to sow good into them? I know I don't! As I am writing this my heart is sinking as I am reminded of how indiscriminately I speak sometimes. I truly hope that the conviction that I feel right now enables me to grow as a son of God.

I have the pleasure of working with one of the most incredible men I have ever met, Steve Burton. I do everything I can to make our company the best place for which anybody could ever hope to work. We are truly considered a destination employer. We have cleaners and managers simply begging to work for us, and I hope we will grow big enough to hire and love them all. Steve is not shy about expressing his gratitude of this environment. I often see clients after he has spoken so highly of our family environment, and even me! The funny thing is, the more he says about me the more I want to say about him. You see how this works? He speaks life into my world, and I speak life into his.

That power becomes a driving force for my improvement. He becomes a physical reference for my Godly pursuit.

I used this example once about the influence of words: Bob introduced me to his friend Mike. Mike was a kind of loud guy that liked to compare himself to people and was not shy about telling how successful he was. Right away I thought to myself, I do not like this guy. I like Bob and was surprised that he chose a friend like this. A week after meeting Mike, Bob came up to me as said "Mike cannot stop talking about how much he enjoyed meeting you". Suddenly I thought to myself, he was really not that bad, really a good chap actually. Do you see how this works, *words* create *influence*! *Influence is power*!

Let me tell you how powerful influence is. Do you realize that every mainstream religion has the exact same formula? Your circle of acceptance equals your circle of influence, there is not choice here! It just happens. Those who accept you will influence everything about you.

"You are the average of the five people you spend the most time with." Jim Rohn

You become who you hang around, it just happens. You have no choice!

Proverbs 13:20
Walk with the wise and become wise, for a companion of fools suffers harm.

The formula is this: circle of influence + truth claim = religion. Every religion, good and bad, has come into existence through this equation. Religion and disagreements over them have caused more death and destruction than almost any other thing in the history of the world. Remember when I speak of Religion I am not necessarily speaking of Christianity, Judaism and Islam. I speak of Religion by the aforementioned formula. For example, by all accounts, the 20th century was the bloodiest in human history. Two major world wars, the Jewish Holocaust, and the Communist Revolutions in Russia, China and Southeast Asia and Cuba. Some have the estimated death toll as high as 100 million. I have been argued with by classifying the genocide of Jews as the scientific process of an elimination an 'inferior race' as an ideology, and not a Religion. However, ideology is a Religion. It starts with a sphere of acceptance, then makes a truth claim, and suddenly you have convinced an enormous amount of people to do the unthinkable with little or no remorse, Religion.

The word heart is a Hebrew word leb or labe, which means courage, will, willingness etc.... We can fairly accurately translate it as emotions. What Solomon is saying here is that what you let in your eyes and ears and out of your mouth will have *everything* to do with your ability to have a pure heart, which is who you are. Remember default positions are revealed during critical life circumstances. What Solomon is saying is, when you need courage, willingness, obedience, discipline etc.... you will be limited by the constant maintenance of your heart. Your circle of influence will dictate 90% of what will contaminate or cleanse your heart.

Like those in Germany, they became easy targets of acceptance of Hitler's evil plans. Because of Hitler's industrial revolution he gained popularity (sphere of influence). The moral compass became easily re-calibrated as Germany's wealthy started thinking, "well he's not so bad, look at our bank account". Hitler was then able to launch his plan of creating a genocide of the Jews in order to protect the "master race". Their eyes went from God to themselves and their wealth. The slow fade enabled them to do things unimaginable to their brother Jews.

There is a simple phrase that stuck with me from the book "Servant" by James C. Hunter. As he explained the phenomenon of Jesus' style of leadership he added something that really helped me... "Fake it till you make it". I later built on that in a LTE (Leadership Training for Executives) meeting. The premise of the meeting was the following: What you think you will eventually believe, what you believe is what you will eventually become.

2 Corinthians 10:5
We demolish arguments and every pretension that sets itself up against the knowledge of God, and we take captive every thought to make it obedient to Christ.

One of the biggest self-built spiritual obstacles is the inability to be accountable for one's thoughts. Again, I see it mostly in Church and in pastors a lot. We become so obsessed with what we look like on the outside that it becomes the end game! The end game is what is on the inside!

Luke 11:39
Then the Lord said to him, "Now then, you Pharisees clean the outside of the cup and dish, but inside you are full of greed and wickedness.

I remember a few years ago hiring a young man, whose father was a pastor. He worked for my company (as a favor to the family that are dear friends of mine) for a short period of time. In that period he almost never made it to work on time and I had several complaints from this very important client. Well, one day he was driving through the business park he was working, not paying attention, and he hit a landscaper with his car. The landscaper was okay, but had to go to hospital by ambulance for a hurt shoulder. Apparently the billy goat that he was pushing was destroyed as well. Instead of seeing the gentleman was okay, he ran. (Default position) He stashed his car at a nearby restaurant and hid out in a restroom. After the management office was informed of the incident, they started trying to reach "X" on the phone. He would not answer his phone and the management figured out quite short order that it was him that hit the landscaping gentleman. Within an hour or two, the police had found in in the restroom crying and encouraged him to come out and deal with the consequences. He did, and went to jail for the night.

The following Sunday morning in service, the pastor's wife quietly hands me a note. "Please don't mention anything about this to anyone here at Church, we really don't want this to get out." This shattered (for the 1,000 time) what my understanding of the Church was… forgiveness, support, love and mercy? It was later followed up by a conversation with his father, the pastor that

123

essentially was explaining to me that it was not as bad as we thought...a simple mistake etc..."Spin". Essentially taking no heartfelt responsibility.

You see the problem here is that the outside of the cup has become more important than the inside. The fact is, our insides are ugly, sinful and in desperate need of a savior. When we make the outside more important, we negate our dependency on our savior, Jesus. Facebook is a notorious avenue for a false projection of one's life. I have yet to see someone post, "I thought about this girl with impure thoughts", or "All I have been thinking about is this new car that I want", or "I cannot believe how awful I spoke to my wife and children yesterday, please pray for my forgiveness and growth". Why? Don't I want people that love me to pray for me?

Guarding your heart is a lot more difficult than controlling the "spin". It is taking full responsibility of your thoughts and actions. Repentance does not activate until it cost you something. I tell my kids all the time: "You don't change until it hurts you that you hurt me." When you replace conviction with justification, you have dethroned God and taken his seat! I hope you are up for the challenge!

Conclusion

What is the most powerful thing in the universe? You! God is within you! You make a nuclear *bomb* look like a firecracker. Your heart is where that power lies. Your grooming, pruning, fertilizing and repenting will yield that power that will make you simply say… My God, My God, My God in whom I TRUST!

I cannot over emphasize the massive importance of guarding your heart. It is the nucleus of your being. Your emotions, passions, security, fear, hope and above all Love comes from it. This begins and ends with who and where you spend your time.

Proverbs 13:20
Walk with the wise and become wise, for a companion of fools suffers harm.

Make no mistake, you are becoming whom you hang around. You are becoming better or worse, not stagnant. There is no such thing as stagnation in this life, it is one or the other. Are you spending time with someone you want to become, or trying to change them? Are you in a relationship with someone that is not going to ever make you better? Are you in a job that is sucking the life out of you? You *are in process*! What is the potential outcome of your current process?

I pray with every morsel of my being that God will touch your heart and encourage you pursuing a personal relationship with him through the Holy Spirit that lives inside of you. It is real, and not a fictitious brainwashing process. There is simply too much evidence to support the Bible's accounts of Christ and what he did for you. If you deny it, you are simply lazy and understudied! I hope that offended you? :-) Please understand this: there is no selfish gain in me writing this book. It has taken me places that have hurt, and created discord in some personal relationships that were very important to me. I knew this before I began. I wrote this book for you. If it cost me everything in order for you gain a fresh and beautiful understanding of how much your Father in Heaven loves you, and wants to be your personal savior and keeper, it was worth it.

I would like to end with this prayer:

Father, we are so grateful for your gift. We are so undeserving and totally insufficient apart from your Grace. Every day we awake may we be reminded of your sacrifice in order for us to have Peace. May we also never let a day go without counting our blessings to the point that we have to stop because there is simply not enough time. I pray that we never call out your name in vain, but awe. Father the gift you gave us in order for us to have the direct pathway to call you Father Abba, is simply matchless and beyond anything we could ever understand. I humbly beg you touch every heart in your unique way in order to help us all get closer and more reliant on your Holy Spirit that lies within sinners and saints. I pray that every time we face adversity that we run to you, and as you promised, we would be comforted. Father we are hurting in some way, but you are the only thing capable of putting us back together. Until we see you face to face…

Amen

The rain descended, the floods came, and the winds blew and beat on that house; and it did not fall, for it was founded on the rock.
(Matthew 7:25, NKJV)

Honor and majesty are [found] in His presence; strength and joy are [found] in His sanctuary.
(1 Chronicles 16:27, AMP)

The glory of this present house will be greater than the glory of the former house,' says the LORD Almighty. 'And in this place I will grant peace...
(Haggai 2:9, NIV)

There is no fear in love. But perfect love drives out fear, because fear has to do with punishment. The one who fears is not made perfect in love.
(I John 4:18)

"If you tether yourself to the past, rest assured it will show up in your future." ~ Aaron Hudson

"Pay attention to the tension, that is God's voice you are trying not to hear." ~ Aaron Hudson

"Take responsibility for everything." ~ Aaron Hudson

"Critical life circumstances reveal default positions, default positions reveal heart conditions, heart conditions are who you are!" ~ Aaron Hudson

"Attitude always precedes Aptitude." ~ Aaron Hudson

"Fear is the bait to all cages." ~ Aaron Hudson

"Forgiveness pays the debt, everything else pays interest."
~ Aaron Hudson

"The heart does not desire what the eye does not see."
~ Aaron Hudson

Made in the USA
Lexington, KY
26 October 2016